California's Chumash Indians

MUSEUM OF NATURAL HISTORY EDUCATION CENTER

PROJECT COORDINATORS
Lynne McCall & Rosalind Perry

CONTRIBUTORS
Rosalind Perry, Lynn Roche, Pam Hoeft, Jan Timbrook,
Patricia Campbell & Nick Miller

ILLUSTRATORS
Anne Powell, Patricia Campbell, Jan Timbrook,
Claire Van Blaricum & Pam Hoeft

JOHN DANIEL, PUBLISHER / 1986

NOTE

The name *Chumash* is derived from the word *Michumash*, the name given to the Santa Cruz Islanders by the mainlanders. It probably means "those who make shell bead money" from the word *'alchum* meaning "money."

Designed and typeset by Jim Cook
SANTA BARBARA, CALIFORNIA

Library of Congress Cataloging-in-Publication Data
CALIFORNIA'S CHUMASH INDIANS.
   Bibliography: p.
   1. Chumashan Indians.   I. Santa Barbara Museum of Natural History.
E99.C815C34   1986   979.4'00497   86-13564
ISBN 0-936784-15-6 (PBK.)

Published by
John Daniel, Publisher
Post Office Box 21922
Santa Barbara, California 93121

Distributed to the trade by
EZ Nature Books
Post Office Box 4206
San Luis Obispo, CA 93403

This book is dedicated to the Chumash people of today
and their valuable efforts to retain their heritage,
and to the memory of
D. Travis Hudson,
without whose inspiration
this work could not have been completed.

Acknowledgments

Project Coordinators: Lynne McCall and Rosalind Perry.
Contributors: Rosalind Perry, Lynn Roche, Pam Hoeft, Jan Timbrook, Patricia Campbell, and Nick Miller.
Illustrators: Anne Powell, Patricia Campbell, Jan Timbrook, Claire van Blaricum, and Pam Hoeft.

We wish to thank the following people without whose help this project could not have been completed:
Thomas Blackburn and Russell Ruiz, for permission to include the Chumash legends; Campbell Grant, for permission to include rock art motifs from *The Rock Paintings of the Chumash*; Travis Hudson and John Johnson, for advice and expertise; Paul Jillson, for his encouragement; Judy Young, for reading the manuscript with an editor's eye; and Lilla Burgess, for her excellent typing job.

We would like to extend a special thanks to Jan Timbrook, for her illustrations, her editing skills and help with the revisions.

We also thank the University of California Press for permission to adapt narrative numbers 1, 2, 5, 6, 13 and 57 from *December'sChild, A Book of Chumash Oral Narratives,* edited by Thomas C. Blackburn, ©1975 by the Regents of the University of California.

Except as noted below, all the illustrations were done by Anne Powell and Pam Hoeft. Jan Timbrook contributed the drawings of the Chumash fishermen, deer hunters, Blackbird Dance and Chumash dance costume. Rosalind Perry drew the map of Chumash territory. Graphic design was done by Pam Hoeft.

Table of Contents

Chumash deer hunters wear disguises made from deers' heads.

The Chumash Way of Life

T HE CHUMASH created a special way of life along the south
central coast of California. Although some other California
Indians had similar customs, no other Native Americans lived in
exactly the same way. Their invention and use of the plank canoe,
their complex village and religious life, and their extraordinary
craftsmanship are what make the Chumash unique. They had their
own distinct group of languages, with eight regional dialects, spoken
from Malibu in the south to San Luis Obispo in the north. These
belong to the Hokan language family, the oldest in California. This
fact suggests that Chumash-speaking peoples were living in this
part of California for thousands of years.

Since the Chumash did not have a written language, we must rely
on archaeologists to tell us about Chumash life before the Spanish
arrived two hundred years ago and imposed a very different way of
life upon them. Archaeologists have found evidence of many ancient
settlements throughout what is now the Santa Barbara region,
including the Channel Islands. Some believe that early hunting peoples were living on the islands as long ago as 35,000 years. Firm
radio-carbon dates stretch back as far as 9,000 years. Complex cultures with Chumash-style artifacts date from some 1,000 years ago.
Archaeologists have much to tell us about gradual change over long
periods of time in the diet, homes, tools, and customs of the Chumash and their predecessors.

When Cabrillo arrived in California in 1542, members of his
expedition wrote the first descriptions of the Chumash people.
Other explorers and missionaries followed, each adding his own
observations to the growing historical record. Important details of
Chumash life during mission and post-mission times were told by
the Chumash who survived into the twentieth century: Fernando
Librado *Kitsepawit*, Juan de Jesús Justo, Luisa Ygnacio, María Solares,
and many others.

From all this evidence, we have learned how the Chumash way of
life reflected the natural world around them. This world was the
source for their food, clothing, homes and tools. It was the inspira-

tion for their religious beliefs, music and ceremonies. They respected and even feared the natural world, for their lives depended on it every day. It could bring them abundance, or threaten them with famine, flood or disease.

Like most California Indians, the Chumash were hunters and gatherers, dependent for their food on the wild plants and animals native to this region. They had a technology—the tools and techniques—for collecting, processing and storing these foods efficiently. And they had a trade network, stretching from the Channel Islands to the highest pine forests, which assured them access to a wide variety of foods all year round. Because of their success in using the natural environment, they did not plant crops of corn, beans, and other vegetables as so many other American Indians did. Nor did they raise domestic animals. They relied, instead, on acorns and other nuts, seeds, roots, bulbs, and leaves from an incredible variety of native plants. They also enjoyed an abundance of fish and shellfish from the rivers and ocean. They were skilled at hunting the plentiful wild game: deer, antelope, rabbits, birds and seals. Beached whales provided an occasional feast. Even such small animals as ground squirrels and grasshoppers were trapped and eaten.

The natural world was also the source for Chumash craft materials and tools. Their homes, beds and baskets were made from locally gathered plants. Their grinding tools, knives, arrowheads and cooking pots were made of stone. They used animal hides and bones for clothing, tools and musical instruments. Shells were important for dishes, ornaments, and even money. No resource was wasted, for these creative and clever people knew that some good use could be found for nearly everything.

Although the Chumash people spent much of their time collecting and using such indigenous materials, food was usually so plentiful that they had ample time for leisure activities: playing games, making music, and telling stories. There was time, too, for religious festivals and for the development of their arts and crafts to the highest standard. The local environment provided such an abundance and variety of materials that the Chumash were able to go beyond survival, to develop a truly unique and fascinating culture.

The Chumash in Historic Times

J UAN RODRÍGUEZ CABRILLO, a Spanish explorer sailing for Spain, came into the Santa Barbara Channel area in 1542. This was the first contact the Chumash people had with any Europeans. Diaries from this expedition reported many friendly visits with the native Chumash:

> "...Here came canoes with fish to barter; the Indians were very friendly...all the way there were many canoes, for the whole coast is very densely populated; and many Indians kept boarding the ships. They pointed out the pueblos (villages) and told us their names," (Bolton. 1925:26).

There were two other known Spanish contacts in 1587 and 1595. The latter was near San Luis Obispo, where the Spanish were attacked by the Indians. The next visitor who related information about the Chumash was Sebastian Viscaíno, who followed Cabrillo's route in 1602. He noted how friendly the Indians were. Viscaíno gave the Santa Barbara Channel its name. These first contacts may have precipitated many changes in the Chumash way of life. New diseases were introduced and religious and philosophical ideas probably began to change.

Over the next one hundred and fifty years contact between the Chumash and the Europeans is undocumented, but meetings must have occurred. By this time, Spain had set up a large, wealthy empire in Mexico and South America and the English and Russians were establishing settlements to the north. This greatly worried the Spanish, who needed control over Alta California (as California and the coast northward was then known) to protect their trade route across the Pacific to the Philippine Islands.

In 1769, Gaspar de Portolá led an expedition to establish settlements and missions in Alta California. It was a combined military and religious effort. The missions were built to convert the Indians to Christianity, while soldiers were posted at presidios and stationed at the missions to protect Spain's political interests. A total of twenty-one missions were eventually founded from San Diego to

Sonoma. Spain felt certain that these measures would protect most of her possessions from any foreign invaders.

During Portolá's travels, he visited many Indian villages and reported that the Chumash were especially friendly, giving the Spaniards gifts of baskets, seeds, fish and acorns. Five missions were built in Chumash territory from 1772 to 1804: San Buenaventura (at Ventura), Santa Bárbara, Santa Inés, La Purísima Concepción (near Lompoc), and San Luis Obispo. As these missions were established, the Chumash found that their way of life changed dramatically and quickly.

The priests (padres) in charge of the missions were successful in drawing many converts to Christianity. Indian labor built the missions and performed the work required for daily life in a Spanish colony. The Chumash were urged to leave their native villages and move to the missions, where they were baptized and taught European trades such as farming, weaving, pottery, ironworking and masonry.

The first Chumash to learn the new way of life went back to the villages and brought more Indians to the missions. Gradually, as the missions grew larger, the population of the villages declined to the point where their religious and social systems broke down. It became difficult to survive in the villages, and eventually most of the Indians were brought into the mission system.

At the missions, the Chumash were trained in European lifeways. Their own political leadership was replaced with complete control by the missionaries. The native hunting, fishing, and gathering economy gave way to mission agriculture and animal husbandry. Dome-shaped tule houses were replaced by rectangular adobe rooms. The near absence of clothing favored by the Chumash was superseded by woolen garments woven in mission workshops. Once indoctrinated into the Catholic faith, the Chumash attended daily Mass, where prayers were recited in both their native tongue and in Spanish.

The Spanish padres enforced a regular work schedule at the missions. On an average day, a bell was sounded an hour after sunrise to announce the commencement of work. Labors ceased by noon, and only an hour and a half was typically worked in the afternoon. Excursions were granted each week to one-fifth of the mission population in a five-week rotation so that Christian Indians could visit their relatives in their native villages. Of course, the mission work schedule varied according to the needs of the agricultural season with longer hours being worked during planting and harvesting. After the fall harvest, most of the mission population was allowed six weeks leave to gather *islay* (wild cherry pits) and acorns, native food plants which the Chumash continued to relish.

The most tragic result of mission life, one which neither native ritual nor the ministry of the padres could prevent, was the heavy loss of life from the dreaded European diseases, such as measles and small-pox. Throughout the colonial period, the Chumash population dwindled rapidly.

After Mexico declared its independence from Spain in 1810, the mission system was seriously disrupted by a lack of money and supplies. Tensions between the Indians and soldiers stationed at the missions flared up into a revolt in 1824. Extra troops were sent in and the Chumash rebels were forced to surrender. Deeply discouraged by the worsening course of events, they could only passively accept their dependent condition.

The mission system came to an end after lasting only about sixty years in the Chumash area. During that time, the once proud and culturally advanced Chumash society had ceased to exist in its original form. Nevertheless, the Chumash had managed to preserve a number of their traditional customs and beliefs.

Beginning in 1833, the missions were broken up by the Mexican government, and their large land holdings passed from the control of the Catholic Church into the hands of private Mexican landowners. The Chumash people now had to make another drastic change in their way of life. The missions no longer offered them a livelihood, but their ancestral villages and hunting and gathering lands were now controlled by new landowners. Most of the Chumash left the mission settlements to seek jobs as domestic servants and cowboys on the big ranches. Others who wished to return to their old way of life had to move far from the coast, to the southern San Joaquin Valley, where they lived a more traditional way of life with the Yokuts and Kitanemuk.

Soon other events occured which disrupted the Chumash life again. California became a territory of the United States, and gold was discovered in northern California. Thousands of Americans traveled west, hoping to become rich. Many new settlers came to the central coast region to farm or to run businesses as cattle buyers and merchants. Even more newcomers arrived after California became a state in 1850.

This large influx of newcomers made life very difficult for all California Indians, including the Chumash. The new settlers wanted land for farms and houses, and regarded as troublesome any Indians who were already living there. Because the laws at that time did not protect the Indians, white settlers could force them off their lands. Racist views of Indians were widespread. Many whites believed that Indians were either "wild savages" to be destroyed, or inferior "diggers" to be laughed at and pitied.

This was a time of great sadness for the remaining Chumash. They were harassed and victimized until they fled their homes and the few remaining village communities. Their families became scattered and afraid even to admit they were Indians. Their children learned to speak Spanish and English instead of Chumash languages. It was difficult for them to get jobs, and many lived in extreme poverty. Thus, the once prosperous and dignified Chumash people became outcasts in their own land, during a period of only one hundred years.

In spite of these great hardships, the surviving Chumash did manage, for a time, to preserve some of their customs. Chiefs were still appointed as late as 1862, when a Chumash woman, Pomposa, was chosen to be Chief of the Ventura Indians at Saticoy. She gave the last traditional fiesta in 1869. Fernando Librado *Kitsepawit*, born at the Ventura Mission, devoted much of his long life to learning about his people's customs, crafts, songs and stories. He traveled from place to place, visiting with the old-timers and trying to help them. When Fernando himself was an old man and the old beliefs and practices were long since forgotten by most Chumash, he passed on his knowledge to the anthropologist John P. Harrington, who wrote down what had been an entirely oral tradition.

One Chumash community did manage to survive down to the present day. It grew up when the Santa Inés Mission was secularized, and some of the Chumash moved their homes from the mission to the banks of a nearby creek. This is now the Santa Ynez

Chumash Reservation, where more than 100 people of Chumash descent are now living. New homes and a community center have recently been built there.

Although no up-to-date census exists, it is estimated that about 1500 people of Chumash ancestry live in Santa Barbara, San Luis Obispo and Ventura Counties today. A growing number of them are becoming involved in an exciting revival of their traditional culture. Some are engaged in craft activities, in which the Chumash have always excelled, including basket weaving, wood and bone carving, beadwork and canoe building. They have also initiated projects to ensure that their sacred shrines and burial grounds are not disturbed.

Once again, they are proud to be Chumash—proud of their history, their spiritual values and their cultural heritage. In spite of everything, the Chumash are not extinct!

The Village Setting

C HUMASH LIFE was centered on the village. There used to be hundreds of villages in Chumash territory, some as large as towns, and some quite small. Villages were usually built on high ground near a good source of fresh water: a stream, lake, or spring.

The largest settlements were located along the coast of the Santa Barbara Channel. They served as political capitals for the surrounding area, and as trading centers for people from the islands and from the mountainous interior. The best location for such a capital town was near the mouth of a large stream. Nearby could be found marshy areas where *tules* for building houses were collected, and safe beaches for launching and landing their many canoes. In larger towns and villages, houses were often arranged in rows, with paths between them.

The chief's house was the largest in the village. He often had many relatives living with him, and he was the only man allowed to have more than one wife. Near his house stood a large storehouse or granary for storing a good supply of acorns and other foods. The chief needed to keep extra food for entertaining visitors and for distributing to any needy people. Some towns had more than one chief: they may have been the heads of important family clans.

There was always at least one sweathouse in every village. The Spanish called the sweathouse *temescal*, which is a word of Aztec derivation. The *temescal* was used not only for cleansing the body, but for masking human scent with the help of aromatic herbs. This was very important to the hunter, especially when he was stalking deer. Since the men did the hunting, they were the ones who used the sweathouse the most. Women and children occasionally used the sweathouses for ceremonies or cures.

The sweathouse was different from a dwelling. It was usually partly underground, with an arching roof of poles, and was covered with mud and thatch. It was entered by a ladder through the roof. A fire was built inside and hot coals or stones provided the heat. Sometimes green leaves or branches were added to produce a humid atmosphere. After sweating, the Indians would leave the sweat-house and plunge into the ocean or a nearby lake or stream.

Each village also had a playing field: a smooth, level area big enough to play such games as shinny, kick ball and the hoop-and-pole game. The playing field sometimes had a low wall built around it.

Another feature of the Chumash village was the ceremonial dance ground in which was located the *siliyik* or sacred enclosure. This was a semicircular area surrounded by a high fence of *tule* mats in which religious rituals were conducted by the priests and sha-mans. The audience sat outside the *siliyik*, around campfires, shel-tered by a large windbreak enclosure of *tule* mats.

Each village had its cemetery nearby. The graves were marked by painted poles. On each grave were placed some of the belongings of the dead person.

There were also special activity areas within the village where tools and artifacts were made. There would be an area where men would make chipped stone tools, such as knives and arrowheads. Sometimes a place would be set aside for the manufacture of canoes, or of shell beads. Often, there was a large outcropping of rock nearby—a bedrock mortar—on which the women cracked and pounded acorns.

Each village traditionally had access to certain hunting, fishing and collecting grounds. Many of them would be nearby, but others might be quite far from the village. Groups of villagers would travel there at certain times of year. They would set up a temporary hunting or gathering camp for a few days or weeks, and then return to their permanent village with their burden baskets filled with extra food.

Sometimes there were disputes between villages over who had the right to certain collecting or fishing grounds. They might decide the issue by having a ritual battle: warriors from the two sides would meet and take turns firing arrows at each other. The battle ended after several men were killed. Other quarrels were settled by taking revenge and burning down the enemy village. But often, the chiefs were able to make peace without anyone getting hurt.

In spite of these occasional quarrels, the villages were usually peaceful places, centered on family life, work, religion, games and music.

Plant Foods

THE CHUMASH people were great hunters and fishers, but an equally important part of their diet consisted of plant foods. Plants were available only seasonally, but many kinds could be stored for later use.

Acorns were the single most important plant food of the Chumash and most other California Indians. Several different kinds were ground, leached, and cooked into a thick mush which is very bland but filling. It was usually eaten with meat, fish, or other dishes. The Chumash also made a mush of wild cherry pits, which had to be boiled for hours in a soapstone pot, changing the water several times to remove the bitter cyanide.

The Chumash also made a thin gruel of cattail pollen; they ate the roots and young shoots of both cattail and bulrush.

Piñon nuts were gathered in inland mountains, lightly toasted in the shell and stored for later use.

The Chumash found the seeds of the *chia* sage tasty and nutritious. They usually toasted the seeds and ground them to a powder, which they ate dry or made into a gruel. Other small seeds of grasses and sunflowers were prepared in the same way as *chia*.

In early spring, the Chumash relished succulent green shoots of miners' lettuce and clover. They ate fruits such as toyon, elderberries, prickly pear cactus and manzanita fresh in season, and soaked some of them in water to make beverages.

The Chumash dug several kinds of edible bulbs and roasted them in underground ovens. The flower stalk of chaparral yucca was also roasted this way.

Sugar was made from the sticky, sweet deposit left by aphids or scale insects on the stems of the large wild carrizo grass. The Chumash ate little or no salt.

BASKET HOPPER MORTAR. *This was used for grinding acorns into meal. The shelled acorns were put into this special basket which has no bottom. It was fastened to a grinding stone with tar. Then the acorns were pounded with a pestle (on the right).*

Clothing and Appearance

OUR UNDERSTANDING of the appearance of Chumash men and women comes from the written accounts of the early Spanish explorers. The following excerpts reveal the first impressions received by the Spanish of the clothing, hairstyles and ornamentation of the Chumash (Grant 1965: 30-31):

> "The dress and adornment of the women was graceful. From the waist down they usually wear two very soft pieces of buckskin, the edges of which are cut into fringes and ornamented with strings of beads, snail shells and others of various colors which give a very pretty effect. One of these skins is worn in front and the other behind. From the waist up they wear (a cape of) fox, otter, squirrel or rabbit fur, oblong in shape and very comfortable. Tying the opposite corners together, they thrust their head and one arm through the (opening) ....They adorn their heads tastefully with necklaces and earrings. Their hair is worn in bangs cut short and combed forward....They trim it daily by singeing it hair by hair with a piece of pine bark so that no hair protrudes. They wear side locks, but the rest of the hair is worn loose, slicked down on top....Their headdress or coiffure gives the women a neat and graceful appearance" (Martinez 1792, in Simpson 1961:53-54).

> "The dress of the men is total nakedness. Some of them have the cartilage of the nose pierced, and all have the ears perforated with two large holes in which they wear litle canes like two horns as thick as the little finger...in which they are accustomed to carry powder made of their wild tobacco. These Indians are well formed and of good body" (Font 1755, in Bolton 1925:250).

"They are well built and of a good disposition, very agile and
alert and ingenious....The men go clothed with a large cloak
made of the skins of rabbit, hare, fox and sea otter; the gar-
ment reaches the waist, the captains only being allowed to
wear it reaching to the ankle" (Fages 1937:25, 32).

The explorers also noted that the men wore a belt or net around
the waist in which they carried various objects, such as knives. They
wore their hair very long, tied up with long strings interwoven in
the hair and ornamented with decorations of bone, flint and wood
(Paez 1542 in Bolton 1925:27).

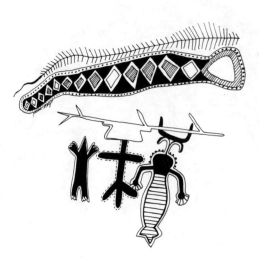

Houses

THE CHUMASH Indians lived in round thatched houses. To make a house, they set willow poles into the ground in a circle. Then they bent the poles toward the center to form a dome shape and lashed them together at the top. They tied smaller saplings around this frame, parallel to the ground, to form a lattice structure. They made an arched doorway, sometimes using large whale rib bones for this purpose.

The outside covering or thatching of the house was bulrush (Spanish: *tule*) or cattails, which they gathered in marshy areas. Large bundles of thatching were draped over the horizontal cross-pieces and tied on to prevent the wind from blowing them off. By starting at the bottom and working toward the top, each layer fell over the one below like shingles, and kept the rain out. At the top of the house a hole was left open for ventilation. In rainy weather, it was covered with a skin.

Each house had a fire pit in the center for heat or for cooking in bad weather. In fine weather, cooking was done outside. Twined *tule* mats were used to cover the doorway in cold weather, or to show that the owners of the house were not at home. In some areas people slept on platforms raised above the floor and covered with mats. The interiors of the houses were sometimes partitioned into rooms by hanging mats.

Single-family homes were usually twelve to twenty feet in diameter, depending on the size of the family. The chief's house was much larger, up to thirty-five feet across. An extended family, including relatives of different generations, shared living quarters.

Uses of Natural Materials

T HE CHUMASH knew many uses for the natural materials in their environment. Most of these materials could be gathered locally. Scarce materials were obtained through trade—items such as steatite, obsidian, sea otter furs, and the red pigment hematite.

Here is a list of some of the most important materials and their uses:

PLANTS	PART USED	USES
Bay Tree	Leaves	Insect repellent; worn around head for headaches.
	Burls	Wooden bowls.
Black Walnut	Nuts	Food.
	Nutshells	Gambling dice.
Ceanothus	Branches	Digging sticks, fence posts, poles.
	Flowers	Lather for washing hair.
Elderberry	Berries	Food.
	Flowers	Tea for coughs, colds, fever.
	Wood	Bows for hunting small game, musical instruments (flute, clapper stick, bullroarer).
Giant Wild Rye & Carrizo Grass	Stems	Arrows; tubes to carry tobacco, which were worn in pierced ears by men; cigarettes.
Indian Hemp	Stems	Most important fiber used for string, nets, cordage.
Juncus (Rush)	Stems	Important basketry material.
Milkweed	Stems	Fiber for cordage, nets.
	Sap	Dried and chewed like chewing gum.
Oak Tree	Acorns	Staple food: ground, leached and cooked into mush.

	Bark	Dye for hides and fishnets.
	Twigs	Used to singe hair.
	Branches	Mush-stirrers, bows, cradleboards.
	Burls	Carved bowls.
Pine Tree	Nuts	Food.
	Pitch	Glue.
	Wood	Canoes, bows.
Sage	Seeds	Toasted for food.
	Leaves	Tea for flu remedy; hunter put leaves in his mouth so deer couldn't smell him.
Soap Plant	Bulbs	Soap; husks made into brushes; crushed for fish poison.
Toyon	Berries	Toasted for food.
	Wood	Arrows, tools: wedges, awls, hide scrapers and cooking implements.
Tule (Bulrush)	Stems	Thatching for houses. Mats for sleeping; sacred enclosure; padding for cradleboard; skirts; sandals; waterbottles.
Wild Cherry (Islay)	Fruit	Food.
	Pits	Food: cooked for a long time in several changes of water and mashed like beans.
Wild Rose	Fruit	Food.
	Petals	Dried, crushed for baby powder; tea used as eyewash.
Willow	Wood	Poles for house framework, cradleboard.
	Shoots	Baskets, seed beaters.
	Bark	Lashing; skirts; chewed as a toothache remedy; tea for fever.
Yucca	Leaves	Fiber for sewing and cordage.
	Rosette	Roasted and eaten.

MINERALS	USES
Asphaltum or tar	Glue and sealant for canoes, attaching points to arrowshafts, mending bowls, waterproofing baskets.
Chert & fused shale (rarely, obsidian)	Projectile points (arrowheads and spear points), knives, scrapers, drills.
Hematite, a red pigment	Paint for body painting, cave painting, canoes; widely traded.
Sandstone	Grinding stones, mortars and pestles, manos and metates; large carved bowls.
Steatite ("Soapstone")	Easily carved and can be heated without breaking; used for cooking bowls and frying pans, pipes, charmstones, effigies, arrowshaft straighteners, beads.
Serpentine	Beads, ornaments, charmstones, "doughnut stones" used with digging tools.

ANIMALS	PART USED	USES
Birds:	Meat	Food (especially ducks, geese and quail).
	Bones	Flutes, awls.
	Feathers	Fletching for arrows, decoration, banners, ceremonial dance skirts and headdresses.
Mammals:		
Deer	Meat	Food.
	Sinew	Bowstrings, backs of bows.
	Bones	Whistles, flutes, tools, beads, fishhooks.
	Antlers	Tools: wedges, flakers for projectile points.
	Hoofs	Rattles.
	Hides	Clothing, hunting disguise (complete with head and antlers).

Bear	Meat	Food (cubs were captured and fattened).
	Hides	Capes for chiefs and canoe captains, ceremonial costume for bear shaman.
Rabbits	Meat	Food.
	Hides	Cut in strips and woven into blankets.
Seals & Sea Lions	Meat	Food.
	Hides	Capes, blankets.
	Whiskers	Drills for making small holes in shells.
	Bones	Tools, pry bars, sweat sticks.
Sea Otters	Hides	Highly valued for capes and blankets.
Whales	Meat, blubber	Food, when washed ashore (not hunted).
	Ribs	Doorways for houses, wedges, pry bars.
	Vertebrae	Stools, mortars
Shellfish:		
Abalone	Meat	Food (pounded in mortars).
	Shells	Dishes, fishhooks, ornaments, beads, inlay decoration.
Olivella	Shells	Beads, "money."
Clams	Meat	Food.
	Shells	Scrapers for preparing basketry materials, adze blades for woodworking, beads.
Fish:	Meat	Staple food.
	Vertebrae	Beads.
	Sharkskin	Sandpaper.
	Swordfish beak	Headdress for ceremonial costume.

The Plank Canoe

THE MOST famous invention of the Chumash was the plank canoe, called a *tomol*. It was very important to their way of life. Without horses or engines, a good, fast boat was the best way to travel and to carry goods from place to place along the coast. The Chumash were great traders and exchanged many kinds of things between their large towns on the coast of the Santa Barbara Channel and the villages on the Channel Islands (Santa Cruz, Santa Rosa, San Miguel, and Santa Catalina). They also used these strong, well-built canoes for fishing in the Channel and for hunting seals, sea lions and sea otters.

Every coastal town had several canoes which went out in the Channel in good weather to fish or to travel to the islands. According to the Chumash Indian, Fernando Librado, "The canoe was the 'house of the sea.' It was more valuable than a house on land and was worth much money. Only a rich man owned such a canoe . . . " (Hudson, Timbrook and Rempe 1978:39).

These canoes were fashioned entirely by hand, with tools made from stone, animal bones, or shells.

"The old-time people had good eyes and they would just look at a thing and see if it was right. No one hurried them up—it was not like the whites. The Indians wanted to build good canoes and they did not care how long it would take. A long time was needed if they were going to make a good canoe....Sometimes the Indians would finish building a canoe in about 40 days, but sometimes it took from two to six months before it was done" (Hudson, Timbrook and Rempe 1978:41).

The best material for making a canoe was redwood. It swells up when it gets wet, and this helps to prevent leaks. It is also easy to work because it is a soft wood. Because redwood trees didn't grow near the home of the Chumash people, they looked for large redwood logs which had floated down from futher north along the coast and had washed up on the beaches as driftwood. If they couldn't find any redwood, they would use pine wood instead. (The word for "pine" was *tomol*, which also meant "canoe" in the Chumash language.)

After collecting the wood, the Indians would split it into long planks, only about three-quarters of an inch thick. Then they would carefully shape the planks, using tools made of deer antlers, sharpened stones, or clam shells. They smoothed the planks with sharkskin sandpaper so they would fit together tightly. Starting at the bottom of the canoe, each row of planks was stuck in place with sticky tar. Then holes were drilled with chert tools and the planks were tied together with rope made from milkweed plants.

When at last the canoe was finished, the Chumash made it quite waterproof by painting it with a mixture of tar, pine pitch, and red ochre color. Beside the red paint, they often decorated the canoes with shiny abalone shells. Then they also had to make two or three long paddles with a blade at each end shaped like a shovel or a horse's hoof.

When they were finally ready to launch the canoe, four men would carry it down to the water's edge. Then they would say a prayer to the World:

Give room!
Give room!
Give room!
Give room!

Do not get discouraged!
Do not get discouraged!
Do not get discouraged!

Help me to reach the place!
Help me to reach the place!
Help me to reach the place!

Hurrah!
Hurrah!
Hurrah!
Hurrah!

(Hudson, Timbrook and
Rempe 1978:133)

When the water seemed calm enough, they carried the canoe through the surf to the deeper water. There they loaded it up, while the captain or owner of the canoe was holding it steady. Then the two crewmen would get in and the captain would get in the stern. The fourth man, still standing in the water, would give them a good push, and they were off—flying across the water "as fast as a man can run " (Hudson, Timbrook and Rempe 1978:137).

These canoes were often very large, even thirty feet long, although some were only twelve to eighteen feet long. The bigger ones could hold up to twelve people, or a great deal of cargo. Besides the captain and crewmen, they often took along a boy or an old man. He would sit in the middle of the canoe and bail out any water that leaked in, using a small basket or an abalone shell.

THE BROTHERHOOD-OF-THE-CANOE

The Brotherhood-of-the-Canoe was a special group of men who knew how to make canoes and how to travel in them across the Santa Barbara Channel. If anyone wanted to learn how to make canoes, he had to ask to be admitted to the Brotherhood. If he were accepted by the others, he would have to make a payment to the Brotherhood. Then they would adopt him as a brother and teach him their secrets.

Members of the Brotherhood lived in all the different canoe ports around the Santa Barbara Channel. Every brother would help any other brother who was in trouble—for example, if his canoe was damaged during a storm. They were some of the richest and most respected people of the Chumash towns. In their fast and sturdy canoes, they could go far out into the Channel and catch the largest fish. They could travel to the faraway islands and bring back heavy loads of food, tools and ornaments. They could even go to Catalina Island to trade for the valuable steatite bowls made there.

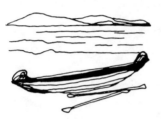

Map of Chumash Territory

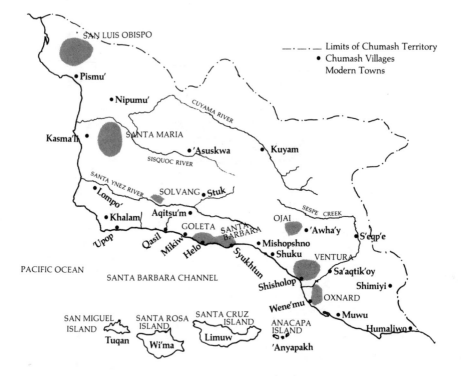

This map shows some of the Chumash settlements of the pre-Mission period, about A.D. 1750. There were many more villages occupied by the Chumash than we have space to show here. We have selected settlements which were in approximately the same location as modern towns, and those where a modern place-name has been derived from the original Chumash name.

Chumash Map and Place Names

The italicized names in the modern name column have been derived from the Chumash place-names. The symbol ' is a glottal stop: a catch in the throat such as in the English expression, "oh-oh." (Reference to Applegate 1975.)

THE CHANNEL ISLANDS

CHUMASH NAME	MEANING OF NAME	MODERN NAME
'Anyapakh	"Mirage"	Anacapa Island
Limuw	"In the Sea"	Santa Cruz Island (in Island language)
Michumash	"Place of the Islanders"	Santa Cruz Island
Tuqan	?	San Miguel Island
Wi'ma	"Redwood"	Santa Rosa Island

CHUMASH VILLAGES

CHUMASH NAME	MEANING OF NAME	MODERN NAME
'Aqitsu'm	"Constant Sign"	Village in *Cachuma* Canyon.
'Asuskwa'	"Stopping Place"	A place on the *Sisquoc* River.
'Awha'y	"Moon"	*Ojai*
Helo'	"The Water"	Village on an island in Goleta Slough.
Humaliwo	"The Surf Sounds Loudly"	*Malibu*
Kasma'li	"The Last"	*Casmalia*
Khalam	"Bundle"	Village on *Jalama* Creek.

35

Kuyam	"To Rest, To Wait"	*Cuyama*
Lompo'	"Stagnant Water"	*Lompoc*
Mikiw	"On the Other Side"	Dos Pueblos
Mishopshno	"Correspondence"	Carpinteria
Muwu	"Beach"	Point *Mugu*
Nakhuwi	"Meadow"	Village near *Nojoqui* Falls.
Nipumu'	"Village"	*Nipomo*
Pismu'	"Tar"	*Pismo* Beach
Qasil	"Beautiful"	Refugio Beach
Sa'aqtik'oy	"Sheltered from the Wind"	*Saticoy*
S'eqp'e	"Kneecap"	*Sespe*
Shimiyi	?	*Simi*
Shisholop	"In the Mud"	Ventura
Shuku	?	The Rincon
Stuk	"Wooden Bowl"	Village in *Stuke* Canyon
Syukhtun	"It Forks"	Village near the beach in Santa Barbara.
'Upop	"Shelter"	Village at Point Concepcion.

Trade and Trails

THE CHUMASH obtained many of the things they needed from their own neighborhood. They built their houses near fresh water, near good places to gather plant foods, to hunt or to fish, and near marshes where they collected the *tule* rushes to make houses, sleeping mats and baskets.

They obtained a large variety of foods and different useful materials, as well as luxury goods, by trading with the people from other villages. There were two ways of trading: barter, where one person traded one thing directly for something another person had, and trading for money. The Chumash often used strings of shell beads for money. The denomination was measured by wrapping the string of beads around the hand. It was said that eight strings of beads were worth a Spanish silver dollar. Most of these small beads were made from olivella shells by the Indians living on Santa Cruz Island.

These Island Chumash often traveled by canoe to the mainland towns to trade their shell bead money and other things they had made (chert blades and knives) for things they needed. Since no deer or rabbits live on the islands, they were very glad to get deer hides and antlers (for tools) and rabbit skins for blankets. They also traded fish, sea lion meat, and sea otter skins for foods that were scarce on the islands: chia seeds, wild cherry, acorns and pine nuts.

The Chumash who lived in the interior valleys and mountains would walk down to the coast and trade for the things they needed: shells and beads, tar, fish and shellfish, sea otter pelts, etc.

The Chumash also traded with non-Chumash peoples from far away. From the Gabrielino of Santa Catalina Island, they got a type of precious soapstone or steatite. The Chumash name for Santa Catalina is *huya*, which also means steatite. This stone was very valuable because it was easy to carve into effigies, pipes, and fancy beads. Large pieces were made into cooking pots *(ollas)*, which did not break when they were placed over a fire, as ordinary sandstone bowls would. Steatite was also used for arrowshaft straighteners, tools which were heated and used for taking the bends out of the wood used in making arrows.

From the Yokuts of the San Joaquin Valley and Tehachapi Mountains, the Chumash traded for obsidian, a volcanic glass rock which makes excellent arrowheads and knives. The Yokuts also traded sugar cakes of honeydew collected from plants and packages of tobacco. They brought these things in carrying nets held on their backs by a rope passed around their foreheads.

The Chumash even traded with the Mojave Indians who lived near the Colorado River, on the California-Arizona border. The Mojave brought pottery, woven cotton blankets, and a red mineral, hematite, which the Chumash valued highly as a paint (used in body painting, cave painting, canoes, and in burials). It took at least two weeks for the Mojaves to walk all the way across the deserts and mountains to the Pacific Coast.

With all this trade, the Chumash prospered; everybody could enjoy a variety of foods, better tools, and many beautiful ornaments.

After many years of trading, the Indian foot trails were worn deep along the hillsides and canyons. When the Spanish explorers came to California in the 1760s, they too followed the same well-worn trails, but now on horseback. And years later, in the 1800s and 1900s, many of the new railroads and paved roads used the same Indian trail system. Today, Highways 1, 101, and 126 in Santa Barbara and Ventura Counties follow the ancient Chumash trails.

But some trails were not suitable for our modern forms of transportation; they were too steep and the countryside too rugged for trains and fast highways. Some of these old trails still remain as country roads or hiking trails. For example, Refugio Pass Road follows the trail which once linked the villages of the Santa Ynez Valley with the coastal town of *Qasil* (Refugio Beach). This was an important center where the inland, coastal and island Chumash could all meet and trade. Special fiestas were held there in its large ceremonial area. Dancing, singing, rituals and offerings took place there, as well as much trading activity.

Social Organization

C HUMASH SOCIETY was divided into three classes: the upper class, the middle class, and the lower class. About one-quarter of the population was in the upper class. The people in this group held all of the important political and religious positions: they were chiefs, canoe owners, craft specialists, and members of the *'antap* cult. Their wealth and positions were usually hereditary.

The middle class included about one-half of the people. They were mainly hunters, gatherers, fishermen and general workers. The lower class was made up of the poor people: social outcasts, lazy and unproductive people, and even some outlaws.

There was no one ruler over all the Chumash people. Instead, each village had its own chief, or *wot* (rhymes with "boat"), who was the leader and moral authority for the village. Women sometimes served as *wots*. The assistant to the *wot* was known as the *paha*. He acted as master of ceremonies at festivals and gatherings. The *ksen* were messengers who traveled from place to place, making announcements and gathering news for the *wot*. The *'antap* was a group of advisors to the *wot*, and they also performed rituals. In this group were various kinds of people—doctors, astrologers, singers and dancers.

Some parts of Chumash territory were organized into provinces, or groups of villages. The village *wots* formed a council which governed the province; one among them was chosen to be the *paqwot*, or "big chief" who ruled over the others. His or her assistant, the *paha*, conducted the ceremonies for the province.

Religious Life

COSMOLOGY

A cosmology is a collection of beliefs about the structure of the universe. The cosmologies of North American Indians are unique and distinct from those of other peoples. The Chumash shared some basic beliefs with other Indian cultures, such as their idea of power, the importance of shamans, and the belief in many worlds.

The Chumash believed that the universe is made up of Three Worlds, which are arranged one above the other, like flat, circular trays. The surface of the Earth, believed to be an island, was surrounded by an ocean. This makes up the Middle World. Above this lies the Upper World, where powerful supernatural beings like Sun, Moon, Morning Star, and other First People live. Below the Middle World lies the Lower World, inhabited by dangerous creatures called *nunashish*. These come up to the Middle World at night, where they are likely to frighten anyone who should chance to see them.

The Chumash believed that, long ago, before the time of humans, the First People lived in the Middle World. Their activities were very similar to those of the Chumash themselves. Then came a great flood, and the First People were transformed into the present plants, animals and natural forces, such as Thunder. Some ascended into the sky to become Sky People, identified as certain stars and planets, among them Sky Coyote (the North Star) and Eagle (Evening Star). After these mythic events, a council among some of the Sky People resulted in the creation of humans.

THE NATURE OF POWER

Power is a central idea in California native religion. It is energy which was scattered throughout the universe when it was created. The Chumash believed that all beings, both human and supernatural, were able to get and use power for either good or bad purposes. Power, therefore, was seen as dangerous. A person could gain extra power only if he or she knew the traditional and secret rules. One could try to get a dream helper—a powerful plant, animal, natural

A whale effigy ('atishwin)

force, star or planet—for assistance. These supernatural helpers included Bear, Eagle, Beaver, the plant *Datura,* Thunder, Whirlwind, various water birds, insects that walk on water, and many more. Each helper could assist a person in various ways, depending on its real and mythic powers. For example, Bear could confer great strength and courage, safety from attack by bears, and skill in dancing the Bear Dance. Other dream helpers could be called for help with craft activities, canoe voyages, gambling, or in times of danger.

In order to get a dream helper, a very special procedure was used. This was usually done only once in a lifetime. It involved fasting and the use of dream-inducing drugs, under the supervision of a shaman. If the seeker was successful and a helper appeared in a trance or dream, the person would then make a charm or talisman *('atishwin)* as a symbol of the helper. One must keep this personal *'atishwin* closely guarded at all times, for if it was lost or stolen misfortune would surely follow. Shamans, chiefs, and other important people could have more than one dream helper, which showed that they were, indeed, the most powerful members of the community. Those without dream helpers, on the other hand, were seen as helpless, fearful, and subject to the will of those who did have power.

The Chumash believed that the most powerful beings in the universe were those who lived in the Upper World: Sun, Moon, Sky Coyote, Eagle, Morning Star, etc. They were thought to have emotions, intelligence and will power, much as people do. They could be unpredictable and use their great power either for good or ill. Sun, for example, could kill everyone by going away, or by making the earth too hot. The Chumash believed that ceremonies were needed to make sure all the power in the universe was kept in balance.

The secret knowledge of how to keep the good and evil forces of the universe in balance was held by a special group called *'antap.* This group included many important members of the village such as the chief *(wot)*, the ceremonial leader *(paha)*, and the shamans (specialists in curing, naming, astronomy, and so on). The *'antap* planned and coordinated the details of life which were most important for the well-being of the community, such as the collection, storage and distribution of food, forecasting the weather, naming children and deciding the date and place of major ceremonies.

CEREMONIES

The two most important Chumash ceremonies honored the Earth and the Sun. Other ceremonies were held for those who had died (the Mourning Ceremony, held every two or three years), for weddings, and for the initiation of a chief.

The *Hutash* ceremony honored the Earth Goddess, *Shup* or *Hutash*,

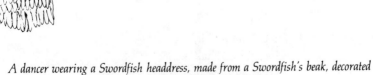

A dancer wearing a Swordfish headdress, made from a Swordfish's beak, decorated with abalone shell. Reconstructed from archaeological finds.

who was worshipped as the source of all food. This was a festival of thanksgiving, which took place just after the time of the acorn harvest in late summer. It was held in the major towns, such as *Muwu* (Point Mugu), *Shisholop* (Ventura), *Syukhtun* (Santa Barbara) and *Mikiw* (Dos Pueblos). Many people came from miles away, even from the Channel Islands, to take part in the ceremonies which lasted five or six days. Such a large gathering was an excellent time for trading with each other and for recreational activities. They enjoyed games in which the villages competed against each other. In the evenings, gambling was popular. An important part of the celebration was the offering of food and shell bead money to the Earth.

The festival included songs and dances which were rich in pageantry, performed in the dance area, around which the spectators were seated on *tule* mats. The location of visiting chiefs among the spectators was marked with tall, painted poles. The *siliyik* was a semicircular enclosure at one side of the dance area, surrounded by a high fence of *tule* mats so the people could not see inside. During the dances, two old men played special ceremonial whistles inside the *siliyik*.

The songs and dances, which could also be performed at other ceremonies or simply for entertainment, were directed at particular plant or animal supernaturals. Some examples are: Blackbird, Swordfish, Seaweed, Fox, Skunk, Beaver, and Bear Dances.

The dancers wore special costumes for these occasions. In the Bear Dance, for example, the dancer had an elaborate feather headdress and carried bundles of feathers. Two bear paws hung from around his neck. The singers, who followed the Bear as he danced past the spectators, carried turtle shell rattles and sang:

"Listen to what I am about to sing.
Listen to my stamping.
I tear the ground up.
Listen to my groaning.

Look! Listen!
He grunts on high.
The ground shakes.
In the night he makes a noise
  like a thunderclap.

> Clear the way!
> I am a creature of power.
> I stand up and begin to walk to
>   the mountain tops,
> To every corner of the world.
> I am a creature of power."

(Hudson, Blackburn, Curletti and
Timbrook 1977: 82-83)

If anybody dared to make a noise during the dance, the Bear might bite him.

The Winter Solstice ceremony was held in honor of the Sun, at the time of the shortest day of the year (December 21 or 22). Great crowds of people would gather for this ceremony. On the first day, all debts from the last year would have to be paid. The next day, the master of ceremonies *(paha)*, who was called the "Image of the Sun," and his twelve assistants, the "Rays of the Sun," would set up a Sunstick. This was a pole about sixteen inches long with a stone disk attached at the top. The disk was painted with twelve sun rays and was angled so that it was in perfect alignment with the sun and thus would cast a magical, circular shadow. Using this power object, the *paha* could symbolically pull the Sun back toward the Earth, to ensure that the annual cycle of growth and harvest would begin anew.

Some cave paintings may have been made by the *'antap* at the time of the Winter Solstice. There are many examples of possible Sun symbols among the paintings which resemble the painted design descriptions of the Sunstick.

Games

THE CHUMASH Indians loved games and contests. They especially enjoyed gambling games. They did not believe in luck, but thought they won or lost because of the involvement of supernatural forces in their lives. They gambled using shell bead money or their prized possessions as the game stakes. Sometimes decisions of political office were made through gambling games. The Chumash Indians also liked games that tested their skills.

Games were played all year long but were played more during the times of major ceremonial gatherings. Some common games were shinny, kickball, hoop-and-pole, dodge rock, marbles, as well as the gambling games such as peón.

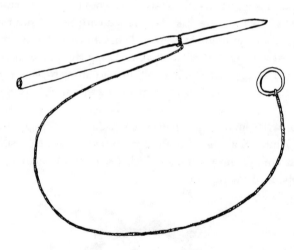

Craftsmanship

T HE CHUMASH were skilled and artistic craftspeople. The *tomol*, or plank canoe, is a prime example of their skill. Many other objects were also made by specialists from a variety of raw materials.

Steatite is a kind of soapstone which the Chumash obtained by trade from the Indians on Santa Catalina island. Steatite is heat-resistant, so it was very useful for smoking pipes, arrowshaft straighteners, and cooking implements such as *ollas* (pronounced "oyas"), or pots, and *comales*. A *comal* is a rectangular slab of steatite with a hole at one end. It was heated in the fire, removed with a stick, and suspended in a watertight basket to cook acorn mush or boil water. It was sometimes also used like a griddle.

A related mineral, serpentine, is also soft and easily carved, so it was made into beads and ornaments and small figures of animals or other things which served as charms. So-called "doughnut stones" of serpentine were slipped over the shafts of digging tools; the added weight made collecting wild roots easier.

Besides steatite and serpentine, other kinds of stone were made into tools. Arrowheads and larger points which were attached to long spears were made from flint or chert, or sometimes obsidian received in trade. Flint was also made into drills, scrapers, choppers, knives and burins (chisel-like tools for working wood). Sandstone bowls and grinding implements were important for preparing seeds for food.

Chumash wooden bowls and plates of different forms and sizes were made by hand so skillfully that they were as well done as those made by machine, according to early explorers' journals. The Chumash also made wooden trays, boxes and ladles. They also used wood for their harpoons and for other fishing and hunting tools.

Animal bones were carved into many different types of useful and ornamental objects such as hairpins, beads, needles, awls for basket-making, wedges and gouges for woodworking, flakers to make stone tools, fishhooks, and whistles and flutes.

Asphaltum, or tar, was another indispensable raw material for the

Necklace made of serpentine beads.

Chumash. They used it to seal their basketry water bottles, which served as canteens. They caulked their canoes, attached the points to the shafts of arrows and spears, and inlayed shell decoration into various objects with it. They also chewed it like chewing gum.

Plant fibers were used to make shelter, clothing, basketry, and cordage. Thick, coarse rope made from Indian hemp was used for ropes and harpoon lines. Thinner string made from hemp, nettle, or milkweed was used for lashing or tying things, and also was made into fishnets and carrying bags.

The Chumash made many beautiful kinds of beads and ornaments from shells, especially abalone shell. But they are best known for their shell bead money manufactured from olivella shells, primarily on Santa Cruz Island. A string of disk-shaped beads measured around the hand was called a *ponco*. The value of a *ponco* was determined by the color and quality of the beads, and it was actually used to buy things the way we use money today. The Chumash supplied most of the shell money used by Indians throughout southern California, making them one of the wealthiest of the California Indian groups.

Basketry

CHUMASH BASKETRY is a unique facet of California's cultural heritage. Baskets have been made in this region since ancient times. No baskets of great antiquity have survived, but we know of them from clues in asphalt, stone, and bone: very old chunks of tar with basketry imprints on them, asphalt-covered pebbles used long ago in waterproofing baskets, and rings of asphalt on ancient stone mortars where basket hoppers once were fastened. Tar imprints and bone awls tell us that typical coiled Chumash baskets probably have been made for at least a thousand years.

Basketry was a life-sustaining, integral part of traditional Chumash culture. The pervasiveness of basketry in daily living in the old days is hard for us to imagine. The Chumash lived in basketry domes, usually made of lashed willow poles thatched with *tule*. They collected acorns, seeds, roots, shellfish, and other foods using woven seedbeaters, coiled burden baskets, twined sieves, and knotted carrying nets. The women leached acorns in baskets, ground acorns and seeds in basketry hoppers, winnowed seeds in basketry trays, and stored food in baskets. Parching trays and watertight boiling baskets were used in cooking. The Chumash ate and drank out of baskets. Water was carried and stored in asphalt-lined basketry water bottles. Basketry hats were also used for measuring in trade. Rabbitskin blankets, women's skirts, and dance costumes were made with basketry techniques. Baskets were used in ceremonies to collect offerings, to hold the sacred herbal water, "tears of the sun," and to wet ceremonial deerbone whistles. For entertainment, Chumash women tossed walnut-shell dice on flat coiled trays. With these dice and gambling baskets, political leaders were sometimes chosen for life. The Chumash slept on twined mats, with rolled-up mats for pillows. Babies were kept in twined cradleboards. Special baskets were made for gifts and to hold treasured belongings. Baskets were burned in honor of the dead. When women were buried, baskets decorated their graveposts.

Early Spanish explorers were most impressed with Chumash

basketry, mentioning it as early as 1587. In the 1790s a later visitor, Menzies, wrote in his journal:

"They had...some curious wrought baskets which were much admired and eagerly purchased....Their baskets are...so closely worked as to hold water....They work in them figures of the most complicated kind; we have seen representations of animals, the arms of Spain, and long inscriptions worked in these baskets by the illiterate people with a degree in exactness that was really astonishing" (Menzies 1924:315, 326).

Pedro Fages, a soldier in the De Anza expedition of 1776, expressed his admiration for Chumash basketry:

"In their manufactures, these Indians...are more finished and artistic than those of...San Gabriel....The women weave nearly all their baskets, pitchers, trays, and jars....The tools of these skillful artisans are only two, the most simple ones in the world, the knife and the punch" (Heizer and Whipple 1971:257).

The De Anza expedition bought so many baskets that several entire villages were sold out. These souvenir baskets were sent back to Spain, Mexico, and Peru, where some of them are to be found today. Later, French, English, Russian, and American adventurers similarly dispersed the baskets.

The onslaught of Spanish and American culture during the periods of missionization and secularization devastated traditional Chumash life. Considering the cultural disintegration that occurred, it is remarkable that Chumash basketry persisted at all. But a few authentic baskets were still being made at the turn of the century. Among the last traditional basketmakers were Candelaria Valenzuela and Petra Rios, both of Ventura.

In the early 1900s John Harrington, an anthropologist for the Smithsonian, interviewed Candelaria, Petra, Fernando Librado and others, who generously and patiently shared what they knew of the once glorious tradition. Most of this information, however, was not disseminated until the 1960s, and much of it has still not been published.

In recent years, several Chumash women and men have continued to make well-constructed coiled baskets. Lacking access to traditional materials and techniques, they have used raffia, yarn, pine needles, and store-bought reed to make contemporary baskets. Today, by studying Harrington's notes and the surviving baskets

A coiled juncus basket, 16-1/2 iches in diameter, with an especially complex design. (Dawson & Deetz, 1965: plate 7-d)

themselves, by finding the plants which were used, and by experimenting with processes and techniques, we are recovering, at least to some extent, the craft of the Chumash basketry. A number of Chumash people, anthropologists, botanists, students, and craftspeople are participating in the project.

Baskets made by Candelaria and Petra survive today, along with many older baskets which have been kept as family heirlooms, preserved in museums, or found in cave caches in the Cuyama Valley and the Santa Barbara backcountry.

Among the most beautiful of Chumash baskets are the exquisitely shaped, finely coiled, globular jars with intricate, all-over designs. The most elaborate are the presentation trays with special designs including, indeed, the arms of Spain and inscriptions. These and other coiled baskets, including the more coarsely woven and minimally decorated utilitarian types, are made with a three-rod foundation of juncus—or sometimes bundles of deergrass (Muhlenbergia) with stitching of split juncus rush (Juncus textilis) or splints of three-leaf sumac (Rhus trilobata). Black-dyed sewing elements were used to make the designs in the coiled baskets, along with the natural colors of the materials ranging from reddish brown to very light buff.

There also exist a number of twined water bottles, made of whole juncus stems or split and twisted tule, lined with asphalt. We have examples, descriptions, and mentions of several other basket types, including openwork twined sieves, twined basins, and twilled wickerwork seedbeaters. Chumash fiberwork includes cordage, netting, and twined matting.

Chumash basketry design is characterized by delicacy and restraint and an unusual, marvelous sense of balance. Most of the decorated coiled baskets have a principal band circling the basket, in from the edge a bit. Edges are often finished with rim ticking, blocks of alternating light and dark stitches. Typical design features are radiating spokes, horizontal bands, and small figures which break up larger light or dark areas. Finishes are neatly tapered.

No doubt there was more diversity in traditional Chumash basketry than we are aware of. Less than three hundred known Chumash baskets exist today. The third largest collection in the world is at the Santa Barbara Museum of Natural History. These baskets have not received the wide recognition they deserve, but are highly appreciated by those who know them. In workmanship and design, Chumash basketry ranks among the most outstanding in North America.

Music

THE CHUMASH have been widely recognized for their musical talent. The anthropologist, John Harrington, recorded many songs and myths of the Chumash people on old-fashioned wax cylinders. Not much was known of the contents of these fragile cylinders, however, until 1978 when Gary Tegler, Research Associate of the Santa Barbara Museum of Natural History, transferred them to new tapes and transcribed the words and music. Tegler was amazed at the beauty of the melodies in many of the songs, just as Harrington must have been when he recorded them. There were lullabies, gambling songs, songs of joy, and songs to teach children the morals of Chumash society.

Songs and musical instruments were used to accompany the many dances presented at traditional festivals, rituals, and ceremonies. The Chumash also played music for recreation and for curing the sick.

Musical instruments included whistles, flutes, bull-roarers (flat sticks held by a string and whirled in the air above one's head to make a humming sound), and rattles.

Songs varied according to the dance they accompanied. Every song had a name and was sung by specially chosen singers. Sometimes dancers would sing while they danced or would play an instrument to the beat of the dance.

Dancers wore special costumes and painted special designs on their faces and bodies for each dance. Sometimes they carried bunches of feathers or wore a wreath of feathers around their heads. The names of some dances were: the Fox Dance, the Skunk Dance, the Arrow Dance, the Barracuda Dance, the Bear Dance, and the Coyote Dance.

Legends

F IVE OF THESE legends ("The Three Worlds," "The Sky People,"
"The Flood," "The Making of Man," and "The Seven Boys Who
Turned into Geese") were told to John P. Harrington, the anthropologist, by one of his Chumash consultants, María Solares. She
was born at Mission Santa Inés and lived in the Santa Ynez Valley
most of her life. She died in 1922 at an advanced age.

"The Chumash Calendar" is based on information given to Harrington by the Chumash Indian Fernando Librado, who was born of
Santa Cruz Island parents at Mission San Buenaventura in 1839. He
later wandered about, seeking work on various ranches, and visiting
the remnants of the local Chumash communities. His memories (as
recorded by Harrington) have proven invaluable to those seeking to
understand and appreciate Chumash traditions.

These six legends have been adapted from *December's Child: A Book
of Chumash Oral Narratives,* edited by Thomas C. Blackburn (1975).

The last legend in our collection, "The Rainbow Bridge," was told
to us by Russell A. Ruiz, Santa Barbara historian.

THE THREE WORLDS

There is this world in which we live, but there is also one above us
and one below us. Here where we live is the center of our world—it
is the biggest island. And there are two giant serpents that hold our
world up from below. When they are tired they move, and that
causes earthquakes. The world above is held up by the great Eagle,
who causes the phases of the moon by stretching his wings (Blackburn 1975:91).

THE SKY PEOPLE

There is a place in the world above where Sun and Eagle, Morning
Star, and Sky Coyote play *peón,* a gambling game. There are two
sides and two players on each side, and Moon is referee. They play
every night for a year, staying up till dawn. In December, when the
year is ended, they count up to see which side has won the game.

When Sky Coyote's side comes out ahead, there will be a rainy year. Sun bets all kinds of food—acorns, deer, wild cherries, seeds, ducks, and geese—and when Sky Coyote is the winner, he cannot wait to get his winnings, but pulls open the door so that everything falls down into this world.

This game involves us humans, too; for when Sun wins, he gets paid in human lives. Then Sun and Sky Coyote argue, for Sky Coyote wants to pay his debt to Sun with old people, who are no longer of any use. But once in a while, Sun wins the argument and a young person may be picked out to die.

Each one of the Sky People has a task to perform: Sun lights the day, Morning Star lights dawn, the Moon lights the night.

Moon is a single woman. She has a house near the Sun's house. Moon and Sun and the others never get older; they are always there.

Sky Coyote is our father. We have great faith in him. He works for us, giving us food and sparing our lives. He watches over us all the time from the sky. He has the form of a coyote—a *big* coyote.

Eagle is up there watching the whole world, too. He never moves; he is always in the same spot. When he gets tired of holding up the upper world, he stretches his wings a little, and this causes the phases of the moon. When there is an eclipse of the moon, it is because his wings cover it completely.

Eagle is Sun's partner in the *peón* game, for they both are believed to eat people. The place where Eagle lives is surrounded by hills and hills of white bones from the people he has eaten. Eagle has no wife or family; he is always called Chief *(wot)*: "He who commands." He is very patient. He is always there in the sky, thinking.

Sun is an *old* man. He is naked, with a feather headdress on his head, and he carries a torch in his hand. In the early morning, Sun carries a torch high and then lowers it a little at a time to make the world hotter. He follows a trail around the world all day, resting three times. When he reaches the west in the evening, he takes his torch and returns home very quickly, going around far to the south.

Sun is a widower. He lives alone with his pets and his two daughters, who have never married. They have aprons made of live rattlesnakes. Sun's house is very big and is made of crystal. It is full of all kinds of animals—bears, lions, elk, deer, wolves, rattlesnakes, birds—all of them tame.

When Sun returns home in the evening, he takes along whatever people he wants. If they are big, he tucks them under his belt, but if they are babies, he tucks them under his feather headband. He arrives home in time for supper and throws the people down in the doorway. Then he and his two daughters cook and eat them. Every day Sun carries off people from this world—every day (Blackburn 1975:91-93).

THE FLOOD

Spotted Woodpecker, Sun's nephew, was the only one saved in the flood. We don't know why the flood came or how it started, but it kept raining and the water kept rising higher and higher until even the mountains were covered. All the people drowned except Woodpecker, who found refuge on top of the tallest tree in the world. The water kept rising until it touched his feet. He cried out to Sun, "Help me, Uncle! I am drowning! Save me!"

Sun's two daughters heard him and told their father that his nephew, Woodpecker, was calling for help. "He is stiff from cold and hunger," they said. Sun held his torch down low and the water began to go down again. Woodpecker was warmed by the heat. Then Sun tossed him two acorns. They fell in the water near the tree and Woodpecker picked them up and swallowed them. Then Sun threw down two more acorns. Woodpecker ate them, too, and was content. That is why he likes acorns so much—they are still his food (Blackburn 1975:94-95).

THE MAKING OF MAN

After the flood, Sky Coyote, Sun, Moon, Morning Star, and Eagle were discussing how they were going to make man. Eagle and Sky Coyote kept arguing about whether or not the new people should have hands like Coyote's. Coyote said that all the people in this world should be in his image, since he had the finest hands. Lizard was there also, but he just listened night after night and said nothing.

At last, Coyote won the argument and it was agreed that people would have hands just like him. The next day they all gathered around a beautiful white rock that was there in the sky. It was so fine and smooth on top that whatever touched it left an exact print.

Coyote was just about to stamp his hand down on the rock when Lizard, who had been standing silently just behind him, quickly reached out and pressed his own perfect hand print onto the rock.

Coyote was furious and wanted to kill Lizard, but Lizard ran down into a deep crack and escaped. Since Eagle and Sun approved of what Lizard had done, Coyote couldn't do anything about it. If Lizard had not made his print, we might have hands like a coyote today! (Blackburn 1975:95).

THE SEVEN BOYS WHO TURNED INTO GEESE

This happened long ago, when animals were people.

There was a little boy whose mother was deserted by the boy's father. After the father left, the boy's mother married again.

One day, the stepfather went out hunting for ducks and fish, and he brought some home and roasted them, for in those days the men did the cooking. The stepfather and the mother ate the fat ducks while the boy sat watching. But they didn't give the little boy anything to eat.

The mother told him, "Go to your father for food!" So the boy got angry and left. He went to look for something to eat—anything would do. At last he found some wild onions and ate them.

When he went home to go to bed, his mother said, "Go out and play." The poor boy went outside and lay down to sleep. The next morning he got up and began to dig for more wild onions. Along came another boy with the same problem: he was hungry, he had no father, and his mother had married again. The two boys spent the night out in the open, and the next day they dug up more wild onions.

Raccoon came along and saw them digging. "What are you boys doing here?" he asked. "Don't you have any mothers?"

"Yes, but they don't want us," said the boys.

Just then a third boy arrived, and he also had a mean stepfather. Raccoon said, "Boys, I'm going to take you someplace else." He took them to a place where another kind of root, which was very good to eat, was growing. He dug some up for the boys.

Pretty soon two more abandoned boys came by and saw that Raccoon was giving the other three boys food. Now there were five boys, and they ate until they were full.

Then Raccoon asked, "Do you boys want to come and stay with me? I live in the sweat-house."

"Fine," they answered. So they went along to the sweat-house where Raccoon built a great fire. After they all got warm, they happily went to sleep.

The next day Raccoon asked, "Boys, aren't you going home for breakfast?"

"Oh, no," they said. "They don't want us at home."

So Raccoon took them to a place where some delicious plants were growing. Pretty soon two more little boys wandered by. Now there were seven of them. They ate and got full.

Then the oldest boy said, "Boys, I'm thinking of going North."

The others said, "Well, wherever you go, we'll go, too."

"What about our poor uncle, Raccoon?" asked the oldest.

"We'll take him, too," said the others.

"Good. Now I'll show you how to do it!" said the oldest.

He collected some goose down and put some on the head and shoulders of each boy. They threw goose down on Raccoon, too.

They began to sing this song:

> "Turn around, like this
> Everyone.
> Turn around, like this
> Everyone.
> Spread out your arms."

The boys began to fly up in the air, around and around the sweathouse. Raccoon came along below, walking on the ground. The boys came back and completely covered Raccoon with goose down. But still he stayed on the ground.

The boys shouted down to him, "You can't go with us, Uncle, though we wish you could." And Raccoon began to cry.

The boys went higher and higher in the air. Soon they were no longer boys, they were geese.

The oldest gave a loud cry, and everyone in the village came out of their houses to look. The seven mothers came out to look and saw their boys were high in the air. The oldest boy's mother reached out her arms toward him and said, "Ah, little son, come down!" But he only flew higher. And all the mothers began to cry. Raccoon was crying, too.

The boys flew around the sweat-house three times. Their mothers shouted, "Come down, little ones. Come down, and we will give you some food to eat." But the boys replied, "Yey, yey, yey," and flew away far to the North. The mothers followed them, crying.

And as they flew North, the seven boys who had turned into geese became seven stars (Blackburn 1975:245-248).

THE CHUMASH CALENDAR: "THE TWELVE"

The year began following the Winter Solstice, around December 22. Each month was thirty days long. Children were named by an astrologer-priest, according to the month in which they were born.

Here are the months of the Chumash calendar, together with the qualities of those born in each month:

JANUARY

"Month of Datura" (a sacred plant, which was highly respected). People born in this month have a great deal of self-respect. They will succeed, if they use their virtues correctly.

FEBRUARY

"Month When Things Begin To Grow." This is a month of rain, which brings forth whatever is there. People born in this month are never sure of anything and are sometimes unreliable. They take advantage of any opportunity.

MARCH

"Month of Spring." Spring leaves do not all come out equally strong, and the same is true of people born in this month. Some are strong and healthy, but many are sick. People born in this month are usually sad.

APRIL

"Month When Flowers Are in Bloom." People born in this month are cheerful and work for the community. They are pleasant, for the season of flowers is pleasant.

MAY

"Month When Carrizo Is Abundant." (Carrizo is a type of cane used for making arrows and tobacco tubes, which were like cigarettes). People born in this month know about good and useful things, like medicine.

JUNE

"Month When Things Are Divided in Half." This is the time of year when people go out in different directions to gather food. People born in this month are sensitive, serious, careful, and respected by others.

JULY

"Month When Everything Blows Away." Plants begin to lose their leaves in the dry summer wind. People born in this month are never at peace. Like the wind, they are always stirring things up.

AUGUST

"Month of Fiesta" (The Harvest Festival). People born in this month collect everything that belongs to them. They are thrifty and good to their neighbors.

SEPTEMBER

"Month When Those That Are Dry Come Down." All creatures who fear cold and water come down to a warmer place, for they have already stored what they need for the winter. People born in this month are careful and watch out for danger.

OCTOBER

"Month of the Great Canoe-Builder." His name was *Sulupiauset,* which means "Very Respected Bear," and he lived on Santa Cruz Island. This is the time of year when canoes had to stay home because of storms at sea. People born in this month will be very rich. They will make shell-bead money. They will roam from place to place, but the world will protect them.

NOVEMBER

"Month When Rain Keeps Us Indoors." People born in this month are never satisfied.

DECEMBER

"Month When The Sun's Brilliance Begins." The Winter Solstice marks the end of winter and the beginning of spring and a new year. People born in this month are inactive when they are young. Later in life, they become active and strong, just as the sun grows stronger.

"The sun gives strength to man to comprehend that man also is a god in the world. For what would this world be without man?" (Blackburn 1975:101-102).

RAINBOW BRIDGE

The first Chumash people were created on Santa Cruz Island. They were made from the seeds of a Magic Plant by the Earth Goddess, whose name was *Hutash.*

Hutash was married to the Sky Snake, the Milky Way. He could make lightning bolts with his tongue. One day, he decided to make a gift to the Chumash people. He sent down a bolt of lightning, and this started a fire. After this, people kept fires burning so that they could keep warm, and so that they could cook their food.

In those days, the Condor was a white bird. But the Condor was very curious about the fire he saw burning in the Chumash village. He wanted to find out what it was. So he flew very low over the fire to get a better look. But he flew too close; he got his feathers scorched and they turned black. So now the Condor is a black bird, with just a little white left under the wings where they didn't get burned.

After Sky Snake gave them fire, the Chumash people lived more comfortably. More people were born each year, and their villages got bigger and bigger. Santa Cruz Island was getting crowded. And the noise the people made was starting to annoy *Hutash.* It kept her awake at night. So, finally, she decided that some of the Chumash

would have to move off the island. They would have to go to the mainland, where there weren't any people living in those days.

But how were the people going to get across the water to the mainland? Finally, *Hutash* had the idea of making a bridge out of a rainbow. She made a very long, very high rainbow, which stretched from the tallest mountain on Santa Cruz Island all the way to the tall mountains near Carpinteria.

Hutash told the people to go across the Rainbow Bridge, and fill the whole world with people. So the Chumash people started to go across the bridge. Some of them got across safely, but some people made the mistake of looking down. It was a long way down to the water, and the fog was swirling around. They got so dizzy that some of them fell off the Rainbow Bridge, down, down, through the fog, into the ocean. *Hutash* felt very badly about this, because she had told them to cross the bridge. She didn't want them to drown. Instead, she turned them into dolphins. So the Chumash always said that dolphins were their brothers.

Rock Paintings

HUNDREDS OF caves decorated with rock paintings, or pictographs, can be found in the Chumash back country extending from Morro Bay to Malibu, and including the Channel Islands. The pictograph sites are usually found near permanent water such as a river or stream, and the more remote caves contain more complex paintings.

The pictographs were not intended as art for public viewing. It is believed that in their rock art the Chumash depicted their concepts of the supernatural world, which was just as real to them as the everyday world of things that could be seen, heard, or touched. Thus, Chumash rock paintings are probably semi-abstract representations of supernatural beings such as Sky Coyote or of things seen in dreams. Some pictographs might record events, but many more seem to represent concepts or ideas.

Although we know very little about the meanings of the pictographs, the fact that similar designs are found in the various caves suggests that they might have had a recognized symbolic meaning. Five basic designs are repeated, including symbols used the world over for fertility, water, and rain. Elaborate sun-like circles are also often found. The most commonly found design is a curved line split on each end. Many times, symbols overlap or run into one another, and sometimes a new pictograph covers an older one. They were probably all painted within the last one thousand years.

The Chumash made their paint from natural materials. Black color came from charcoal or a soft, black mineral. Iron oxide made a range of colors from dull red-purple and deep red to bright orange and yellow. White paint was made from diatomaceous earth found near Lompoc. The Indians traded for paint materials which were sometimes prepared into compressed, standard-sized cakes.

Paint cups were made from stone, fish vertebrae, or shells. The cake of paint was ground and mixed with water, or perhaps with juice of milkweed or wild cucumber seeds, animal oil, or whites of birds' eggs to make the image more permanent.

The paint was spread onto the cave walls with brushes made from soap plant, yucca, or animal tails. Sometimes designs were drawn directly onto the cave wall with the lump of pigment.

Where to Go to Learn More About the Chumash

CARPINTERIA CITY HALL CHAMBERS, 5775 Carpinteria Ave., Carpinteria, CA 93013. *Chumash paintings.* (805) 684-5405

CARPINTERIA VALLEY MUSEUM OF HISTORY & HISTORICAL SOCIETY, 956 Maple Ave., Carpinteria, CA 93013. *Chumash artifacts; local history.* (805) 684-3112

CHUMASH PAINTED CAVE STATE HISTORIC PARK, San Marcos Pass (Highway 154) to Painted Cave Road. *Chumash cave paintings.* Contact: Santa Barbara Museum of Natural History (805) 682-4711; California Department of Parks and Recreation, Gaviota Area Administration. (805) 968-0019

HOLLISTER ADOBE MUSEUM at Cuesta College, Highway 1, San Luis Obispo, CA 93401. *Chumash artifacts and exhibits.* No telephone. Open Sundays 1 to 4 during October to May.

LA PURÍSIMA MISSION STATE HISTORICAL PARK, 205 N.H.—RFD Box 102, Lompoc, CA 93436. *Extensive displays of mission life in reconstructed buildings. Self-guided and docent-guided tours.* (805) 733-3713

LOMPOC MUSEUM, 200 S. "H" Street, Lompoc, CA 93436. *Chumash artifacts; local history.* (805) 736-3888

LOS ANGELES COUNTY MUSEUM OF NATURAL HISTORY, Exposition Park, Los Angeles, CA 90007. *Anthropology and natural history; guided tours for school groups.* (213) 744-3341

MISSION SAN LUIS OBISPO MUSEUM, Monterey and Chorro Streets, San Luis Obispo, CA 93406. *Chumash artifacts and exhibits.* (805) 543-6850. Open daily, 9 to 4, 9 to 5 in summer.

MORRO BAY MUSEUM OF NATURAL HISTORY, State Park Road, Morro Bay, CA 93442. *Chumash exhibits, docent presentations, docent-guided tours.* (805) 772-2694. Open daily 10 to 5.

OJAI VALLEY MUSEUM & HISTORICAL SOCIETY, 109 S. Montgomery, Ojai, CA 93023. *Inland Chumash and local natural history.* (805) 646-2290

SAN BUENAVENTURA MISSION MUSEUM, 225 E. Main St., Ventura, CA 93001. *Exhibits on Chumash and local history; site of early Mission.* (805) 648-4318

SANTA BARBARA HISTORICAL SOCIETY, 136 E. De la Guerra St., Santa Barbara, CA 93101. *Guided tours available.* (805) 966-1601

SANTA BARBARA MISSION, Upper end of Laguna St., Santa Barbara, CA 93105. *Self-guided tours; local history.* (805) 682-4713

SANTA BARBARA MUSEUM OF NATURAL HISTORY, 2559 Puesta del Sol Rd., Santa Barbara, CA 93105. *Exhibits on Chumash and North American Indians; natural history. Guided tours, talks in the halls, classroom talks.* (805) 682-4711

SANTA BARBARA PRESIDIO, 122 E. Canon Perdido St., Santa Barbara, CA 93101. *Historical exhibits.*

SANTA INÉS MISSION, 1760 Mission Dr., Solvang, CA 93463. *Site of early mission.* (805) 688-4185

SAN LUIS OBISPO COUNTY HISTORICAL MUSEUM, 696 Monterey Street, San Luis Obispo, CA 93406. *Chumash artifacts and exhibits.* (805) 543-0638. Open Wednesday through Sunday 10 to 4.

SANTA MARIA VALLEY HISTORICAL SOCIETY MUSEUM, 616 South Broadway, Santa Maria, CA 93454. *Chumash artifacts and exhibits.* (805) 922-3130. Open Tuesday through Saturday 1 to 5, Sunday 1 to 4.

SANTA YNEZ INDIAN RESERVATION, Santa Ynez, CA 93460. *Tribal meeting hall, Indian bingo.* (805) 688-7997.

SOUTHWEST MUSEUM, 234 Museum Dr., Highland Park, CA, 90042. *Anthropology and Indian museum.* (213) 221-2163

VENTURA COUNTY HISTORICAL MUSEUM, 100 E. Main St., Ventura, CA 93001. *Exhibits on Chumash and local history. Tours and educational programs available.* (805) 653-0323

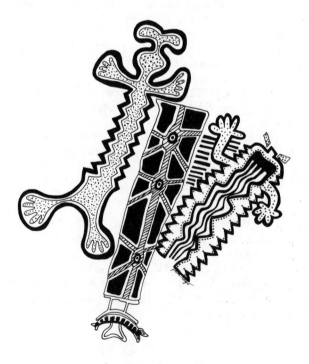

Chumash Word List

SINCE THERE were several Chumash dialects, the words here have been taken from *Whistler's Interim Barbareño Chumash Dictionary*. The spellings have been adapted by Jan Timbrook according to the method of the linguist Richard B. Applegate.

The symbol ' is a glottal stop—a catch in the throat as in the English expression, "Oh-oh."

'alapay	sky
'alishaw	sun
'antap	member of religious cult
'ap	house
'atishwɨn	talisman, effigy
ch'ich'i	child
'eneq	woman
haku	hello
helek	hawk, falcon
'ɨhɨ'y	man
khus	bear
ksen	messenger
mimi	finger or toe
'o'	water (for drinking)
paha	festival leader
qshap	rattlesnake
shup	land
siliyɨk	sacred enclosure in the dancing ground
tomol	canoe
wot	chief

Colors:

akhimay	black
'o'wow	white
tasin	red

The Chumash numbers indicate a base 4 number system, rather than a base 10 system like ours. Note especially the relation between the words for 1 and 5, 2 and 6, and 3 and 7.

Numbers:

1—*pak'a*

2—*'ishko'm*

3—*masikh*

4—*sku'mu*

5—*yit'ipak'a*

6—*yit'ishko'm*

7—*yit'imasikh*

8—*malawa*

9—*spa'*

10—*k'eleshko'm*

Bibliography

Applegate, Richard B. 1975. *An Index of Chumash Placenames*. SLOCAS Occasional Paper 9, San Luis Obispo County Archeological Society.

Applegate, Richard B. 1978. *'Atishwin: The Dream Helper in South-Central California*. Anthropological Papers 13. Ballena Press. Socorro, NM.

Blackburn, Thomas C. 1975. *December's Child: A Book of Chumash Oral Narratives*. University of California Press, Berkeley.

Bolton, Herbert E. 1924. *Spanish Exploration in the Southwest, 1542-1706*. Charles Scribner's Sons, New York.

Clarke, Charlotte Bringle. 1977. *Edible and Useful Plants of California*. University of California Press, Berkeley.

Davis, James T. 1961. "Trade Routes and Economic Exchange Among the Indians of California." *University of California Archaeological Survey Report, No 54: pp. 1-71.*

Dawson, Lawrence E. and James J.F. Deetz. 1965. "A Corpus of Chumash Basketry." *Annual Report, No. 7: pp. 193-276.*

Faber, G. and M. Lasagna. 1980. *Whispers from the First Californians*. Magpie Publications, Alamo, CA. Published in paperback and in a special teachers' edition.

Fages, Pedro. 1937. *A Historical, Political and Natural Description of California*. University of California Press, Berkeley.

Geiger, Maynard, O.F.M. 1960. *The Indians of Mission Santa Barbara*. Old Mission, Santa Barbara.

Grant, Campbell. 1965. *The Rock Paintings of the Chumash*. University of California Press, Berkeley.

Heizer, Robert F. and M.A. Whipple. 1971. *The California Indians: A Source Book*. University of California Press, Berkeley.

Heizer, Robert F. and Albert B. Elsasser. 1980. *The Natural World of the California Indians*. California Natural History Guides, No. 46. University of California Press, Berkeley.

Hudson, Travis, Thomas Blackburn, Rosario Curletti and Janice Timbrook (Editors). 1977. *The Eye of the Flute: Chumash Traditional History as Told by Fernando Librado Kitsepawit to John P. Harrington*. Santa Barbara Museum of Natural History, Santa Barbara.

Hudson, Travis, Janice Timbrook and Melissa Rempe (Editors). 1978. *Tomol: Chumash Watercraft as Described in the Ethnographic Notes of John P. Harrington*. Ballena Press and Santa Barbara Museum of Natural History.

Hudson, Travis and Ernest Underhay. 1978. *Crystals in the Sky: An Intellectual Odyssey Involving Chumash Astronomy, Cosmology and Rock Art*. Ballena Press and Santa Barbara Museum of Natural History.

Hudson, Travis (Compiler). 1979. *The Chumash Indians of Southern California: Selected Readings.* Reprints of articles on the Chumash, organized into twelve chapters. Printed by the Office of the Superintendent, Santa Barbara County Schools.

Hudson, Travis and Jan Tinbrook. 1980. *Chumash Indian Games.* Santa Barbara Museum of Natural History.

Hudson, Travis and Thomas C. Blackburn. 1982-86. *The Material Culture of the Chumash Interaction Sphere.* Ballena Press and Santa Barbara Museum of Natural History. 5 volumes.

Hudson, Travis. 1982. *Guide to Painted Cave.* McNally & Loftin, West, Santa Barbara, CA.

King, Chester. 1971. "Chumash Inter-village Economic Exchange." *The Indian Historian, 4:pp. 31-43.* Reprinted in *Native Californians, A Theoretical Retrospective,* edited by L.J. Bean and T.C. Blackburn, Ballena Press, 1976.

Landberg, Leif C.W. 1965. *The Chumash Indians of Southern California.* Southwest Museum, Los Angeles.

Librado, Fernando. 1979. *Breath of the Sun: Life in Early California as Told by a Chumash Indian, Fernando Librado, to John P. Harrington.* Edited with notes by Travis Hudson. Malki Museum Press and the Ventura County Historical Society.

Martens, Pamela. 1973. *The History and Culture of the Chumash Indians of Southern California.* Santa Barbara County Schools.

Menzies, Archibald. 1924. "Archibald Menzies' Journal of the Vancouver Expedition." *California Historical Society Quarterly, Vol. 2, No. 4: pp 265-340.*

Niethammer, Carolyn. 1974. *American Indian Food and Lore.* Collier Books, New York.

Simpson, Lesley Byrd (Translator and Editor). 1961. *Journal of José Longinos Martínez: Notes and Observations of the Naturalist of the Botanical Expedition in New and Old California and the South Coast, 1791-1792.* Santa Barbara Historical Society and Howell, San Francisco.

Webb, Edith Buckland. 1982. *Indian Life at the Old Missions.* Reprint edition. University of Nebraska Press, Lincoln.

Whistler, Kenneth W. 1980. *An Interim Barbareño Chumash Directory.* Unpublished manuscript on file at the Santa Barbara Museum of Natural History.

Books for Children About the Chumash

Buff, Mary and Conrad. 1966. *Kemi, an Indian Boy Before the White Man Came.* Ward Ritchie Press, Pasadena.

Falk, Elsa. 1953. *Fog Island.* Wilcox and Follett, New York.

Falk, Elsa. 1959. *Tohi: A Chumash Indian Boy.* Melmont Publishers, Inc., Chicago.

Hoffmann, Eleanor. 1965 & 1981. *The Charmstone.* Illustrated by Campbell Grant. McNally & Loftin, Santa Barbara.

O'Dell, Scott. 1960 & 1973. *Island of the Blue Dolphins.* 1960, Hardback edition: Houghton Mifflin Co., Boston. 1973, Paperback edition: Dell Publishing, New York.

O'Dell, Scott. 1976. *Zia.* Houghton Mifflin Co., Boston.

Rambeau, John, Nancy Rambeau and Richard Gross. 1968. *Chumash Boy.* Field Educational Publications, Inc. San Francisco.

Shannon, Terry. 1963. *Wakapoo and the Flying Arrows.* Illustrated by Charles Payzant. Albert Whitman and Co., Chicago.

Whipple, Mary Anne and Nancy E. Heizer. 1962. "Surprise from the Islands." in *The First Californians.* Illustrated by Virginia Seeger. Peek Productions, Palo Alto.

CALIFORNIA'S CHUMASH INDIANS

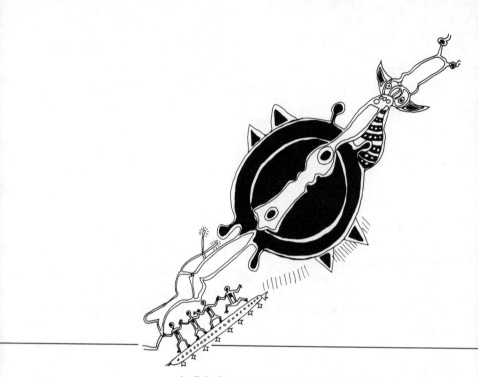

A PROJECT OF THE SANTA BARBARA